EXCLUSIVE TV RIGHTS

One night with rights over the TV
(remote control included)

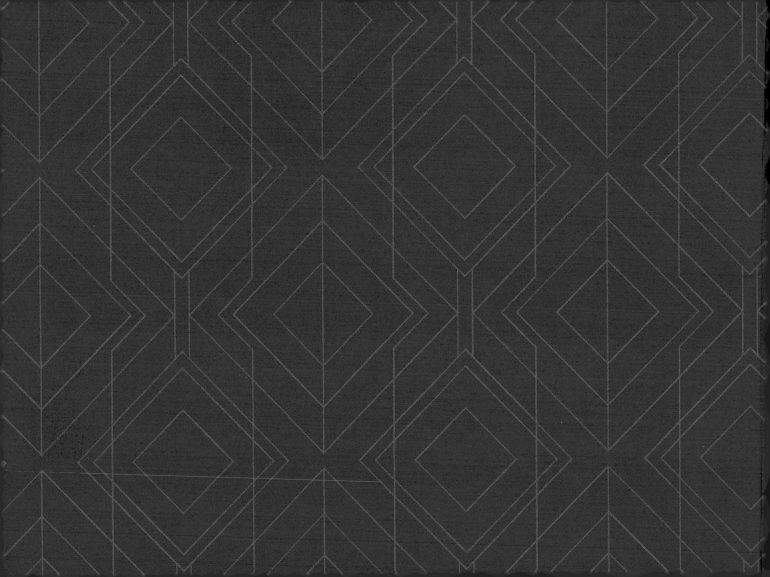

To: _____

From: _____

Date: _____

Message: _____

_____

_____

BREAKFAST IN BED

FAMILY BONDING

A family activity of your choice (the whole family will participate without complaints)

MOVIE NIGHT

You choose the movie; I'll make the popcorn!

BODY MASSAGE

A 10-minute massage of your choice:
back, neck, feet, hands

FREE HUG!

RELAXING BUBBLE BATH

I'll fill the tub and will not disturb you!

NAP TOGETHER

An hour-long nap together

STORY TIME

One hour of exchanging stories or reading books together

FAMILY SCRAPBOOK

I'll help you collect our best family photos to print!

CLEAN BEDROOM

One day of keeping my bedroom clean and tidy without complaints

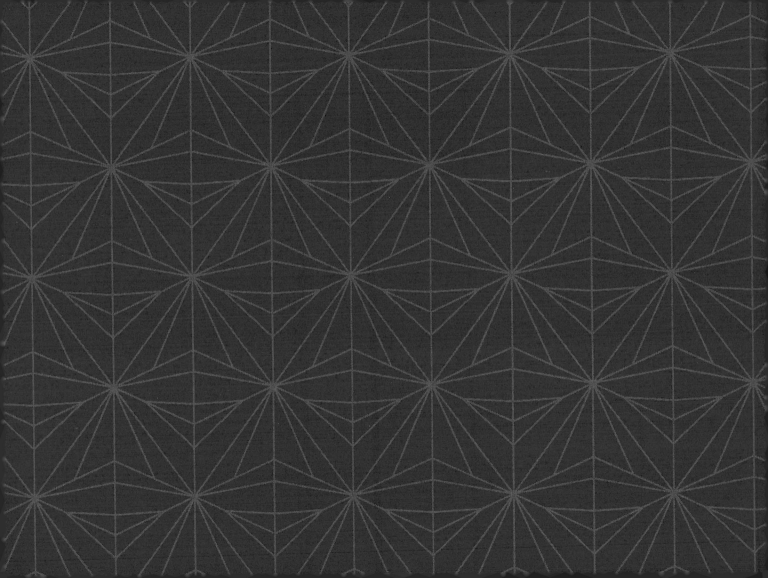

BAKING DAY

An afternoon of baking together

NEW ADVENTURE

Let's take a trip to a place we've never been!

ROMANTIC DINNER

A romantic dinner for just you and daddy.
I'll set the table!

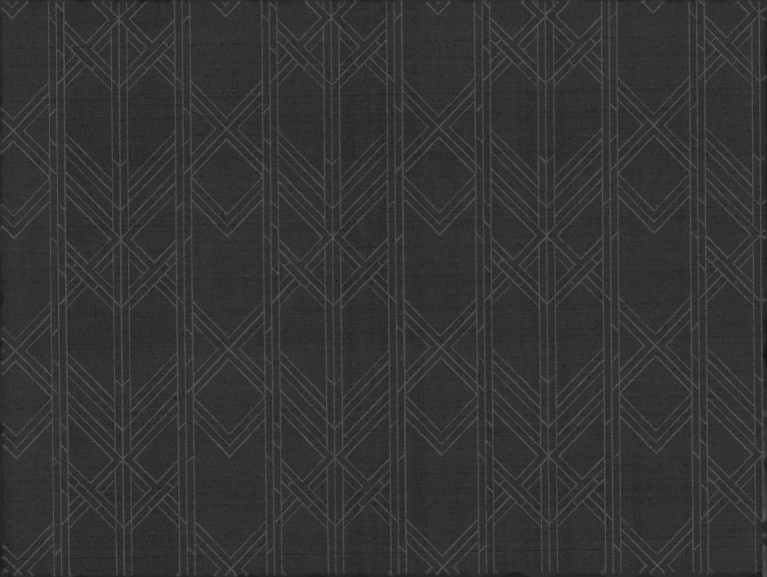

SHOPPING SPREE

An afternoon shopping together

SET the TABLE

I'll set the table tonight!

TRASH DAY

I'll take out the trash today!

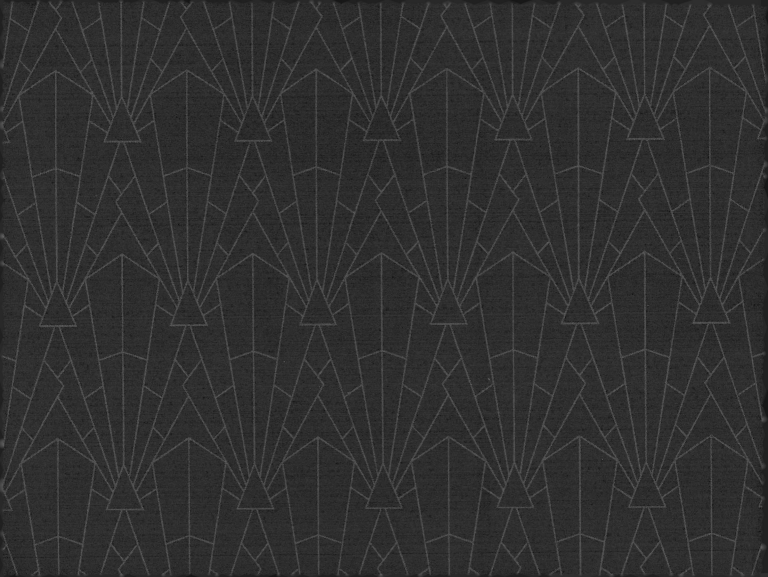

UNPLUGGED

One day without electronics

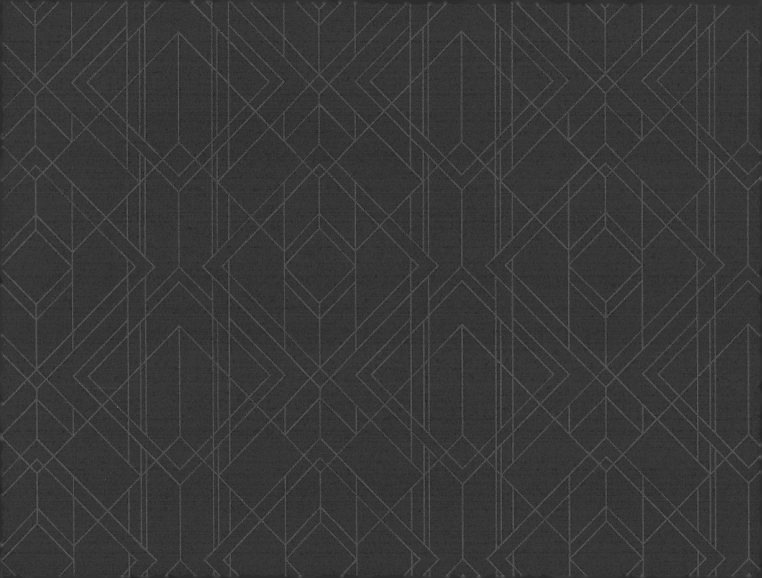

TAKE A STROLL

Your choice of a morning
or evening walk together

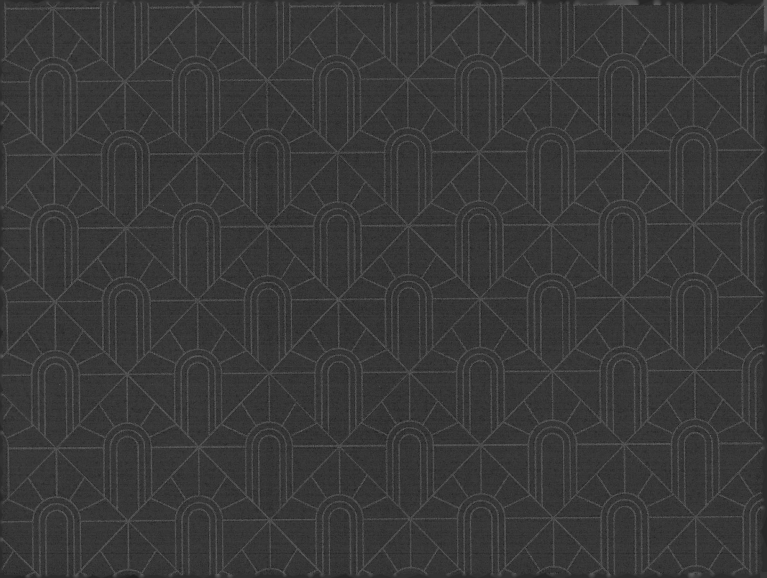

NAP TIME

An hour-long nap without disturbance

ICE CREAM DATE

One afternoon eating ice cream together

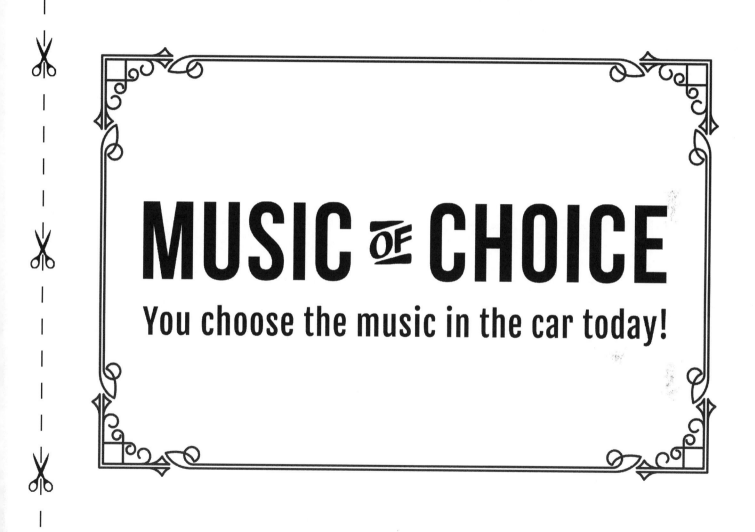

MUSIC OF CHOICE

You choose the music in the car today!

NO ALARMS

One morning without setting the alarm clock.
I can't disturb you!

SOUS-CHEF

I'll help you cook dinner tonight!

GAME NIGHT

One evening of family board games

PICNIC DAY

An afternoon picnic with food and a red checkered tablecloth

DIY DAY

One afternoon working on a household project together

ARTS & CRAFTS

An afternoon making arts & crafts together!

TEA PARTY

An afternoon of tea (or talking) with your friends.
I'll help you prepare everything!

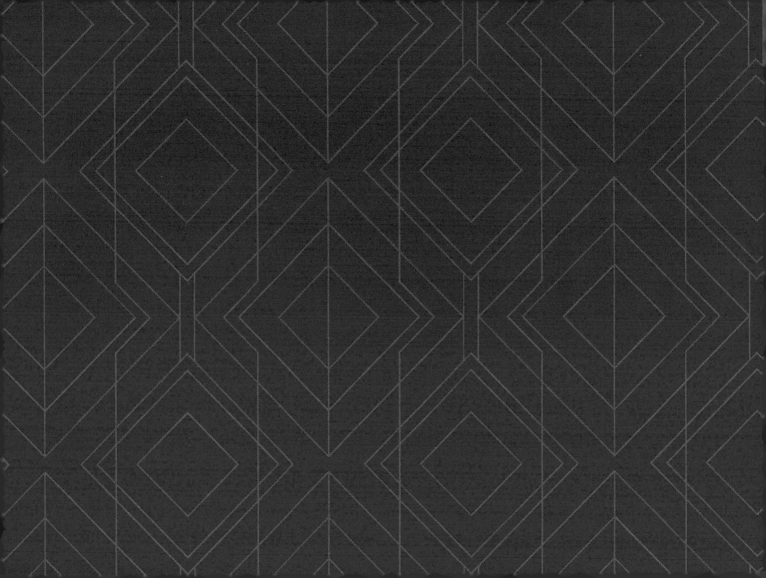

MOMMY'S LITTLE HELPER

I'll help you with anything you need today
(no complaints)

HOUSEHOLD CHORE

I'll do one of your chores today!

WATER ᵀᴴᴱ PLANTS

I'll water the plants this week!

STARGAZING

A night of stargazing together

BLANKET FORT

One night building a blanket fort to sleep in

GET SPORTY

I'll play any sport with you today!

ENJOY THE SUNSET

An evening admiring the sky together

BIKE RIDE

NO COMPLAINTS DAY

One full day without complaints

GARDEN HELPER

I'll help you in the garden
(or yard) today

BEDTIME STORY

I'll read a story to you tonight!

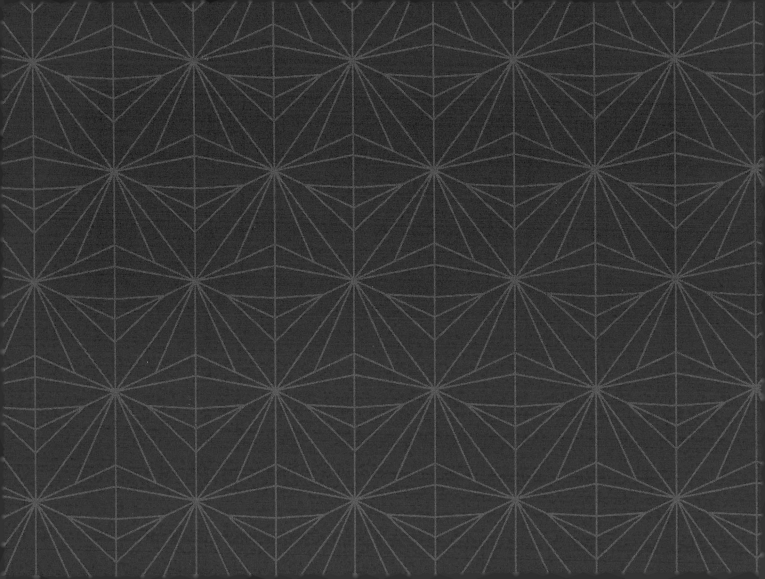

PIZZA NIGHT

We can order in or make it ourselves!

DESSERT NIGHT

I'll make you a dessert of your choice!

FAMILY OUTING

One afternoon spent outside
with the whole family!

FOOT MASSAGE

One 10-minute foot massage

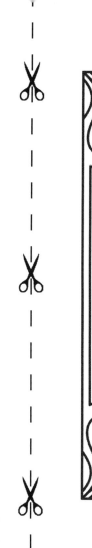

MAKE THE BED

I'll make your bed today!

SPA DAY

One day of pampering.
I'll paint your nails or fill a bubble bath

DAY OFF

A whole day doing nothing, just resting

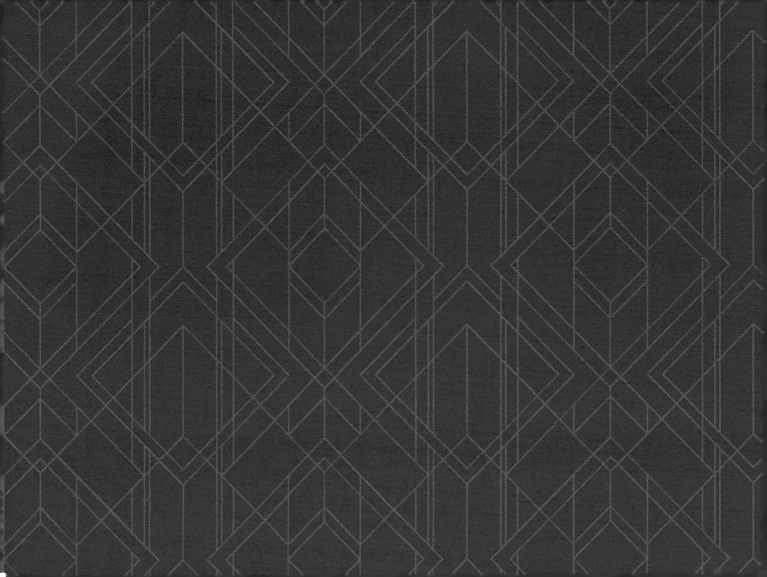

WILDCARD

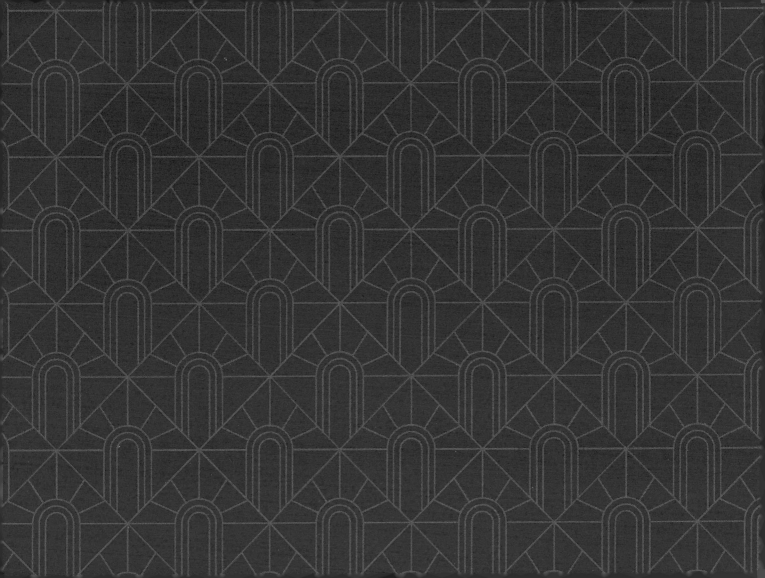

PHOTO SHOOT

A session of taking pictures together

Printed in Great Britain
by Amazon